"And what if someone were to offer you her girlhood and her motherhood, her hidden knives and her soft places, her earliest Afro-Puerto Rican memories and her current pandemic-scape strategies? What then? In *black god mother this body*, Raina León offers what a god mother should offer, a portal to infinite divine possibility, a safe space to learn something new, a multi-faceted generosity. These are poems that mother, mentor and mend and break open again. Leon offers us everything and so we have to decide. What will we do with it?"

– Alexis Pauline Gumbs, co-editor of *Revolutionary Mothering: Love on the Front Lines* and author of *Undrowned: Black Feminist Lessons from Marine Mammals*

---

Mothering has never been easy. And learning to mother oneself back to wholeness and healing while also trying to mother one's own children even harder. In Raina León's collection, however, we are able to see motherhood, and in particular Black motherhood, in all its fullness and complexity, with all its joys and fears in all its tenderness and trauma wrapped in the language of poetry and prayer only a true priestess like León could conjure. *black god mother this body* is a soft and sharp meditation on Black motherhood, colorism, identity, ancestry, and what it means to heal and nurture our inner child. In this striking collection of lyrical prose poems, fragments of memories, and colorful collages, León explores what it means to mother our past and present selves, our children, our memories, and our ancestors even in the face of unspeakable trauma, violence, and uncertainty. When she thinks she can't find the language to express or make sense of these mother wounds, León keeps cleaving and pruning away at her own past until she can get to the root of what it means to mother well, always wondering: is memory the dance of mourning and love that survives long enough to bloom?

– Jasminne Mendez, author of *City without Altar*

---

"A masterful ode to lineage and futures. A deeply personal unearthing of both the whispered and the unspoken for so many of us existing as woman, Black, immigrant, mother, feminist."

– Sherisa de Groot, founder of Raising Mothers

---

*black god mother this body* is rich experience with the expansiveness of the overlapping identities contained in a singular Black woman. The language is a conjuring. The conjure is a poem. A poem is life. Life is breath, pumping heart, sinew and gristle animated by spirit. Life is given by the mother. Raina León gave this book life. The poems and snippets of memoir have teeth. The collages have eyes. The subject matter has bones and muscle. All together - a beautiful soul rises into becoming a most cherished friend. This book is a journey, a healing, a hint at the ability to render trauma poetic. It resists the stagnation of antiquated foolishness about identity. It revels in its own Self so deliciously, you're compelled to join.

– Christina Springer, author of *The Splooge Factory*

Enter this book and watch a woman bloom – with love, with fire, with the grit of life. Raina J. León offers a glimpse into the space of a Black woman's body where old cultures collide with new ideas and the god in her rises from within. Power comes when a woman, turned mother, feels a threat looming over her children with the realization that "this country will kill you if you're not looking and even if you are." This collection is as striking visually as it is crafted with original artwork amplifying the soul of the text. With language and music set to the rhythm of the heart, León's *black god mother this body* is a deeply intimate and powerful celebration of the body and its blessings.

– Amanda Johnston, writer, artist, and founder of Torch Literary Arts

Dr. León's work is a vast and vibrant, multivocal and interactive journey exploring the spiritual and ancestral magic in our bodies. In *black god mother this body* we enter a world where the enduring interconnectedness of being, the "gone and not gone," is our strength, but not without the realities of fear. This book asks questions and meditates with us as we consider the frailty and power of mothering, and of being a child.

– Natalie Graham, author of *Begin with a Failed Body*

With *black god mother this body*, Raina León offers us poetics that feel like collective memoir, for all of us in the lineage of "people murdered slow." The slivers and snippets of memory and confession range a lifetime of being daughter and granddaughter, niece, mother, wife, scholar. This collection is a delicious, intimate and transgressive exploration of complex identity; having read it, I feel fresh and whole.

– adrienne maree brown, author of *Emergent Strategy*

León transcends time and space by taking us through a journey of the intergenerational: her ancestral roots, childhood, pregnancies, and motherhood. This collection intertwines the language of the spiritual, emotional and physical while tackling issues of colorism, racism, patriarchy, wellness, and healing. *black god mother this body* is a calling of reflection and embodiment immersed in life and death during a time of cosmic and earthly shifts.

– Dara D. Mendez, PhD, MPH, maternal and reproductive health professor, epidemiologist and advocate

# black god mother this body

Raina J. León

BLACK FREIGHTER PRESS

First Edition, 1st Printing

ISBN 13: 978-1-955953-01-6

Cover Art & Design: Amy Law

this manuscript includes cueing images that are accessible through the app HaloAR. just download the app, HaloAR, and scan. what comes is home and loving and a spirit that reaches to yours.
1. download the HaloAR app (www.lightup.io/haloar)
2. follow me (username: rainaleon, collection name: black god mother this body)
3. scan the cuing image

Black Freighter Press
San Francisco, California

https://www.blackfreighterpress.com/

for all my foremothers and forefathers and beings before

standing in gratitude
to my mother, dr. norma d. thomas, and father, eddie león
and my children, raffaele and aurélia

you are my living areyto to atabey
you invite me to walk as ancestor at the crossroads
of all of what came and what will come and what is and is

# table of contents

# awe / augmentee

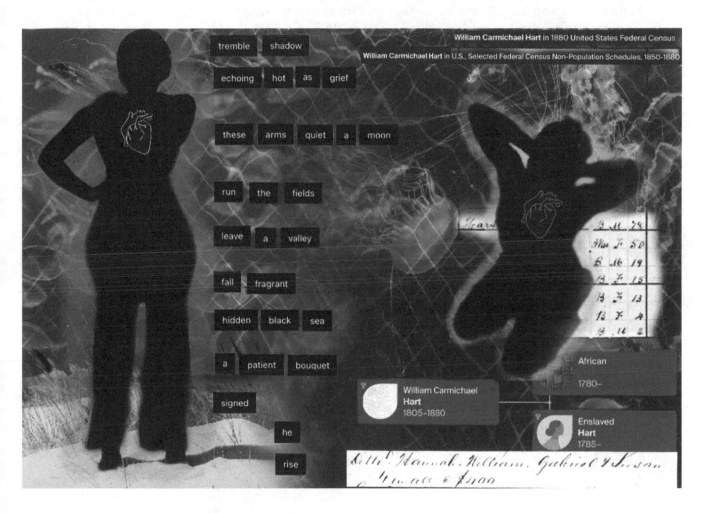

**from the adyton**

nyx who stood at creation's dark dawn, blinks her eyes into a wind whisper and takes human form, fills its fleshy folds with languor. she widens the hips with death, shimmies her swagger so those who see long for an end that starts in her. from her ear lobes, she hangs pearls to counter the tacky tar allure of her eyes. her scent blooms in summer-sweated jasmine. she lives beyond ocean or light, beyond time's witness of dust mounding into the body that entangles with body and abrades, some night after many nights, into dust. she sparked creation in dream and holds it thrumming to bleat. she perches maternal, at the edge devouring. her skin prickles with an ever-primed mother fury. *don't. touch. my. baby.* not his hair. not her body. not their anything. not them. what is not hers, that she has borne and not borne? nothing can be touched and truly known. she most definitively is black, god and feared by gods, loved for her whole night breaking. open.

**testimonio**

*for kamilah nisha moon whose name means perfect life*

i want her to be seen
      no ver
            campos de sangre coloreados por pop
      pauso                ese maldito sonido
      gone and coming through           ay bendita

i want her to not see
      ser vista
      slow revelation of light
overlapping ribbons
          giratoria de oro      green curl    black glimmer a shine    and a hat
      resplandor de pulso    manera de warming her good center
        y siempre
      así que she sleeps in the night campanadas de canciones
tranquil firsts

i want her to be querida
      no por los fuegos artificiales      intoxicantes internos
        all our memories    su vida una luna brilliante    y cortante
        treasured on aged tree-knot tongues forever

no i want her safe and saying my name
like a hip dip secret to the right      just right groove
      not boxed in shining gray
      pero es
        y no está
here and yet is
        here

**what plastic and steel teaches**
> after *five beauties rising: fannie mae* and *five beauties rising: dot,* by willie cole

most of my childhood i hopped
from one plastic mat to another

i imagined them islands
over swampy moats

this my inheritance
the cleansing

each week
my mother would shampoo the carpet

at nine i started ironing
at six each morning

my uniform over the metal face
covered by cloth sprayed-easy starch

what lessons was my mother teaching in what clings to metal
what releases its hold

in the museum i see those boards again
flattened down by the heavy press

of roughed truck wheels
the pressures of world beyond four walls

who dragoons with creased precision
who menaces with starched powder to ring

all the engraved frustrations on a hidden face
under padding set to keep straight

press the wrinkles through steel
and hard metal pocks for steam

a face can be a ship
pressed in ash and grime

riding a frozen paper sea
black and grey against the white

can you see the bodies curled
fetal within the frame of clean

the dirty death and chains
defiant in print

whiteness as background
for a black story

my grandmother learned to clean
she taught my mother to press

even bedsheets to stiff boards
they rattle white walls with voice

listen my mother taught me
to iron a collar crisp

to strip even invisible bacteria from carpet
to clean to pristine and be clean

i only once burned my shirt
with steel eyes

fixed open
and i wore it

so i could see

**nearly five thousand**

on the phone, my father tells a story
of my great-grandmother's sister,
how she could read your spirit in cigar smoke,
and i imagine her lip curl to suck in breath,
the wrap of sun-cracked pucker around tight leaves
to blow a power beyond body through packed tobacco
onto the faces of belief. i did not know her.
some blood power must persist. how to conjure thousands,
what herbs and smoke must rise to see them
among split trees, flopping blue tents,
the black mold mounding to its own glory.
and what of we who scatter, flamboyán seeds,
defiantly burning our own blooming?
we must offer our smoldering through burnt red and gold,
rush into the ether to throng our people murdered slow
by lack:  lack of the electric to run respirators,
lack of milk to flush babes to relaxed sleep
that only the newly born
and elders granted a final ease must know,
lack of clean water to echo our clean amidst the dirty politic.
they. will. rise.
and we will rise together,
twine through silver moss and side-winding ceiba.
i am calling them. we call them.
what was split by wind and hurl rain
made stronger like callouses on fractured bones,
summoning collagen body gold.
we will wear smoke and dark night to fuel our guerrilla tactics,
defend nuestra isla from the invasion that comes.
these are columbuses who use capitalism
like they used disease against the tainos, kill us
with debt, the lack,
to steal land for their leisure.

how the devil delights in playing *capicú* on our bones.
we call them, call the bones to rise and shake,
exchange uselessly flung towels for hauntings.
the devil does not know the danger the living can do
riding a tidal wave of spirit.
we all know how to summon,
starting with our own. thousands gone and not gone,
and we are millions marching machetero.
siempre, siempre pa'lante.
nothing will stop our rising
from even cracked foundations.
nada.
the coquí are already singing.

### blackety black black solstice cleave

*after andrea chung, proverbs 12:22*
*"lying lips are abomination to the lord: but they that deal truly are his delight."*

she is two girls overlapping in time, la negra (o la india, depending on the voice) y la blanca. there is a girl who weeps in this story. there is a girl who watches shirley temple dance while she sits on her father's lap and laughs.

one girl, an innocent memory; the other laughs, too, and doesn't know fear and shame come next. she grows into a woman no one believes.

what do we believe? what hides in the image reflected from the glass: behind a white girl dancing with bojangles in black and white, in front a girl and her father.

there is a black girl who will try to kill a black boy, because he is a light-skinned boy and a vessel for colorism and racism and white supremacy and patriarchy. she doesn't have the names for that. she will try to kill her sweet little brother, who reminds her, in her womanhood of her own son's shy tenderness, how she could have squelched it. she wants to be free, because she knows she already is.

i am the girl who knew joy and knives. i am not the weeping girl with testimonies.

*

what does titi have to teach me?

    her whole mass is the sacrifice:

        the lessons to fight for a black feminist liberation written in what she could not live herself,

    the rules were different and so she lived within them.

                black and ever not.

there is a picture of her wedding, still a girl herself, in a puffy white princess dress. my grandmother, with her cropped red hair, stands at her right hand; my grandfather, smooth and brown, his hair slicked back in a black wave, at her left. they do not smile, but their eyes do. they stand next to a multilayered cake my grandfather had made with his own hands, perfectly smooth and glossed fondant. layered in white. this is a lie.

*

before my husband and i board a plane to go to our co-ed baby shower, i tell him that much of my family will come, including titi. i tell him she is bound to say some locura; his job is to be the wall and keep me away from it. he says, "i don't know what you are talking about. she's always been nice to me." i say, "you are white." the pronouncement is simple. what i don't say is that this is how i know i am supposed to feel i have become successful in her gaze: i am educated, i married a white man (a european no less), and i am pregnant with a boy.

on the plane, i wish i could have a shot of rum. i long for it.

my son kicks within me any time music enters his pulsing water world. he reminds me he is there. and that he will be here. two boys overlapping in the spiral of time.

*

at the shower, she talks about feminism in the new world, how proud she is of me for my education and that i travel, how in her day they never would have had a co-ed baby shower.

first, i think this is what i have always wanted: finally to be seen.

second, that she must be on drugs.

next, that maybe her daughter or granddaughter have had the honest conversation with her in ways i never could. feminist anything so new in the mouth i have studied my whole life.

she tells me the women of our family have never had trouble giving birth. don't all prospective mothers need to know that their labors will be smooth, and so i feel seen in this way; i breathe easy. i welcome that my husband does not need to be a wall. perhaps my whole seeing of her has been wrong. my whole life wrong.

**menú**

arroz con gandules
asopao de pollo
ensalada
perfectly sliced aguacate

we line up. i hear her say to her daughter, "aren't you going to serve your husband?" how quick the return! how minute the fissure!

this is what my mother was told to do when my parents first partnered, nearly 50 years before. the women waited on the men and ate when they were done. the scraps. my mother only did that once, the first time she met my grandmother, out of love for the woman who birthed her man, who loved him first. after that, my grandmother served him, because my mother wouldn't.

it's nearly 50 years later. titi's daughter has herself been married nearly 25 years. she responds, "he can serve himself."

*

at the shower, another titi, this one gladys, makes me café con leche, the color of the inside of my wrist and sweetened nearly to caramel.

her love, magnificent, intimate, warm, una bendición.

titi gladys is not titi.

\*

when i was a child and started school, it was titi who would pick me up from the bus. i remember
the walk to her house. we would pass the plastic-covered couches en la sala and sit at the table in an
all-white kitchen. a snack. homework. a nap in the stale and sterile room of my older cousin away at
college, her nearing graduation brother in the next room, while titi watched her soap operas in hers.
always pristine and still, everything in its place. there were pictures of my cousin all around, her face
that of a sweetened angel. i have always admired her, the girl titi adored and treasured.

eventually, my mother would come to pick me up, and so a day ended. i remember being bored and
internally riotous at the regularity of routine. i had no brother or cousins to play with like at my
grandmother's house, no television to watch, no dogs to tease. i never saw her backyard to run in it. i
had to be careful. i walked lightly. even when i slept, i slept small and contained.  i also slept safe.  this is
important.

the routine ended when she returned to work, and i learned that a woman could raise children or work
in the world, how rare it was to do both.

*

she and tío are my brother's godparents. when we were children, they would come to pick him up, leaving me behind. he went to watch the fights on television or out to dinner. he went many places with them that i don't know. they showed him generosity and care. i remember once they bought him these white hess trucks scripted over in green. tío said, "if you don't open them, someday they'll be worth something" to my brother, a child. to be worth something, one should not play. to have value, it should be observed in its preciousness.

my brother played. he was still worth something.

i was bitter and poisoned as uncooked yautía.

i remember only these gifts from titi: a keychain from puerto rico (an island to which i belonged, but to which i had never been); a t-shirt, also from puerto rico; and a white cabbage patch doll in a white tennis skirt (though i am not white and have never played tennis). all of these were worth something and symbolic of hopes that were not mine.

i was always left behind. to be included would have meant more.

*

i am the madrina of two little girls. i never leave their siblings behind. i claim them as my godchildren, too, though we have not been consecrated in that way. i do this because of how i felt for years. generosity is seeing the whole, how a child wants to be drawn into circle, not pushed out of it.

one of them calls me titi. she once tried to call me by my first name, asserting an authority in naming, and i said to her definitively, "i am titi raina or titi. you don't call me by my first name." i will always be titi. this, too, is a generosity that even in my reflection on the name, i am pulling my titi close.

*

"you need to start wearing makeup." a little lipstick and blush, but not like a puta, she tells me, after she picks up my brother and me from school and walks us home. she always stays for an hour or so while she watches her soap operas.

i am around 11 years old.

i do not know what a puta is. i just know i am not supposed to be one.

what i am supposed to be is never explicitly defined.

\*

between the time with titi and my mother's arrival home, we have a few hours alone. latchkey kids.

we are told not to answer the phone or the door.

that's when i nearly kill my brother.

he is a boy, never told to make himself up, how not to be a puta. he is a boy, never told who or what to be.

*

titi is not my only titi. the first and only time i met my titi ada in puerto rico, really my great aunt, after time spent in the living room to share stories, then she walked us to a room, the entire space an altar to san lazaro, orisha of healing in catholic robes. to say his real name is to invite judgment and destruction. titi ada told a story of how, when she was dying, she prayed to san lazaro to heal her body and in exchange, she would honor him. he did.

in the story i tell now, san lazaro did heal her but he took his praise and her mind. in dementia what she remembered as all her past slipped away, astral, to worship him. this she knew until she died. what i know is that she was beautiful and lovely and loved me at first sight. i belonged in her heart and home.

what we remember. who we forget. i never forget titi. the name is a box of films i once lived.

*

i ask titi to teach me spanish once when i am in elementary school. she teaches me la mano, los dedos. the hand and the fingers. these are the only words.

*

i am boricua of an old stereotype, who dances and dances with fists and can dance until the knife makes you bleed. i learned these things very young. in the times between titi and mami, i tried to kill my brother with a knife for no reason. a snap of a nail once. i can't remember the others. he was faster than me and strong, would always run and hold his door against my weight, until i slid the knife below. for years, he slept on his back, his arms primed above him as if in a push-up, ever ready to rush to push at the door.

i did that.

he was a sweet little boy. he is now a loyal and brilliant man. he represented what i did not have the language to fight. i had time and fists and access to kitchen knives.

when i told my mother this story in college while my brother laughed in confirmation, she said, seriously, "raina, i would have gotten you help."

what help could she have given me, the root of my desire to kill not being about my brother but about colorism and internalized racism made manifest in family interactions and patriarchy and its demands in the mouths and actions of those i loved most?

i am an academic; i can theorize it now.

my brother and i, forged in steel, we are very close. we often laugh inappropriately about death, violence, and survival. there was a story where my father breaks out two axes from his locker when he was a security guard on a college campus ... and the one about a stabbing at a party and the one ...

don't worry. i don't have a knife collection anymore. i have theories.

*

at thanksgiving one year, at my grandmother's table, mami visiting her family in uniontown and my papi, brother and i with the boricua side in philadelphia, titi gives me advice.

i had just talked about applying to graduate school, how i was thinking of schools in new york. "you need to go to miami. marry a nice cuban. there's too much black in the family. all these león men marry black women." my mother is black. i am black. in cuba, they had one of the biggest forced migrations of enslaved africans so they certainly black. and in puerto rico, i know from doing genealogical research and tracing race, generations and generations of our ancestors are black, de color, negro. yes. we blackety black black. and taino and spanish and walking survivors of colonization and oppression, resisters just in being.

i remember putting down the knife and moving to a separate room. i have never challenged her. always accepted her violence. out of respect for an elder, i suffered disrespect. my brother and i shifted our eyes to papi. he ate his chicken, sucking the bone. he hadn't heard anything untoward.

when we told mami what titi had said, there was a war of silence against my father for days.

*

at a black student union meeting in college, my friends talk about colorism within the black community. i speak of the great heaviness and added persecution i feel being dark-skinned. in the mirror of my friends' eyes, i see that i am not dark-skinned, that they do not understand how i can feel so ostracized and attacked within my own family.

i am the only afro-boricua in the room.

*

what conclusions can i make about this particular diasporican identity, shaped as it is by american generational legacies of struggle and resistance, the centering and multidimensionality of our black lives despite white supremacy and the impact of migration and the legacies of racism and colorism and genocide and revolutionary struggle from my father's people, titi's people? what does it mean to be black, afro-boricua, diasporican, woman, mother, me?

2—Que el contrayente *Felix Llui Nogueras* es hijo *reconocido de Camito Nogueras, natural de Cayey, difunto, y de Bernarda Leon natural de Aguas Buenas, Soltera, domestica, vecina de*

**salsipuedes or leave if you can**

y la contrayente *Cornelia Correa y Adorno* es hija *legitima de Isaac Correa, y de Antonia Adorno, casados naturales de Trujillo Alto, industrial y domes ca y vecinos de Puerta de Tierra*

ante el Sacerdote, *Pablo J. Roch* C.S.S. se celebró el matrimonio *religioso*

de *veinte y cuatro* años de edad, de estado *soltero*, de profesión *toreedoi* natural de *Cayey* y avecindado en la casa número *33 4* de calle *Salsipuedes*

*veinte y cuatro* años de edad, de estado *divorcia* de profesión *torcedora*, natural de *Trujillo Alto* y avecindada en casa número *331* de la calle *Salsipuedes* de *Puerta de Tierra*

\*

i have become obsessed with genealogy. i discover in scanned puerto rican church records of baptisms, marriages, and deaths who were the mothers and fathers of whom and who their parents were. find the right record and i leap back two generations. my obsession leaks into the dawn hours. i thank the god of the church of latter day saints for missionaries, the imperialists of faith, whose desire to record the names of those who were to live in heavenly bliss has led to a bounty of records no hurricane can erase.

i trace names. places. race.

we have always been black. indigenous. black.

*

"cleave to your husband, the bible says."

when my grandmother died, she bequeathed her clothes to charity. she wanted those who had nothing to receive gifts her flesh no longer needed. my other aunt prepared her clothes to give, placing them with care on hangers. titi's husband arrived to the house, i learned, and began taking them off the hangers and stuffing them into bags. my aunt responded about my grandmother's wishes, and he replied, "what do you care? juanita's dead." a cruel pronouncement, the reconfirmation that her mother was dead broke my aunt to weeping. he continued stuffing his bags to sell her clothes at a flea market. they could be worth something. a wish was worth nothing. when censured by the family, titi said, "cleave to your husband." punto.

*

cleave means to hold close. it also means to split or sever, especially along a natural line or grain.

\*

titi says, "you are the real family". i must be in my mid-20s then.

my grandmother has just come to our house to pray. she had a dream and so engaged in a visitation to the homes of all her children. we take out rosaries that we have not handled in years and certainly not at home. this is the ceremony of beads and bones. we do what she says and gather in the living room for a shared prayer, five decades of the rosary, and then my grandmother offers her blessings in spanish to each person gathered:  papi, mami, my brother, and me. titi has come with her and sits close, her knees nearly meeting my grandmother's. a triangle shape of body. she translates each blessing my grandmother offers.

santa maría

rosario santo

misterios gozosos hasta los misterios gloriosos

have you see an ascension today?

mothers, what is your assumption plan?

if you don't know the prayers, mumble vowel sounds, emphasizing the soft a and soft e

if you don't know the songs, find the key, wait until the second verse, and hum low in rhythm.

this is how you prove you are worthy of blessings.

follow along. if you keep your head down, you don't have to close your eyes.

for some reason, we talk about my half-siblings, born before and after my parent's marriage, children i did not know about until i was 15 (my older brother and sister) and 21 (my younger brother and sister – the '80s were a crazy time for my father). we are in my living room, and titi says after the blessings have ended, the last blessing on the family as a whole, "but you are the real family. you are the real children."  this is a translator's addition, the meaning only titi's. my brother does not speak spanish well enough to know my grandmother does not say this.

perhaps this is supposed to be a generosity from titi; it is a schism, one which is generationally familiar. did she find comfort in this for herself? my grandfather had two children outside of his marriage, too. his father before him did the same, many times. did she once say to the mirror, "i am the real daughter, the real oldest," as if to give herself more validity and authority, claim a greater love, though his first daughter is older than her, and her brother, born after, given more stature  in the family as the first son, the namesake. boys go into the world and lead. for girls of a certain time, the world is home – anything outside is madness.

*

for hundreds of years, my family's world was bounded by small communities in puerto rico (cayey, aguas buenas, santurce/cangrejos, rio piedras, trujillo alto). look at enough scans of church records and you can go back, on one branch or another, to the 1800s, sometimes even before. it's when the priests were tracking the baptisms of enslaved peoples, their baptisms a way to prevent them from buying their own freedom since a saved soul was worth more, that my people disappear. i wouldn't have been able to identify them assuredly anyway. most of those baptized received the names joseph and maria.

joseph and maria in exile, carried there by a ravenous ship instead of the docile donkey. backs split in cane.

in blackness, we persist even in the resistance to water; in whiteness we toxify.

from archival records i learn that in 1946 my grandmother climbed into the belly of a ship, the marine tiger, with titi who was only 10 months old at the time. she went out into the world, a world in which she would be seen as white and her husband as black. their marriage still illegal then.

i am an academic, looking back on ships.

i feel barbs behind my eyes.

*

as i write this at a farm called smoke, my son is 11 months old. nearby there is a river.

the farm is an hour north of seattle. i am here to teach a workshop, but i find myself living in sense and memory. i think about art at the museum of the african diaspora in san francisco, far from here while in this ozone-electric place. a piece in which memories seem to be pressed into sugar that looks like glass panes made of amber. over time, even in the chill of the museum, inevitably the sugar melts revealing beds, bible pages, scores, rice, patterns erased from moment to moment. blackness encased in the sugar that enslaves, how it melts away and reveals the freedom striving and resilience that was always there.

i am there and here. i see my life through a melting lens.

smoke rises and dances with spirit.

in this place, i learn a friend has committed suicide. rd. he is gone and i ruminate on a world that could not hold him.

this is a performance in living grief. i look up and see coils of rope.

am i pressed into caramelized sugar, a broken window pane in a house melting away?

what are the names of the birds that chirp from the hidden boughs beyond the reach of rustic buildings? robins, wrens, woodpeckers, others. i give over my vision

smoke rises and dances with spirit. still the body long enough and you can see the air swirling with breath unloosed, not bound to this sack that decomposes to starstuff and bone. breath as distinct from whisper or atmosphere. this air is a performance in grief, as in, performance, this is how grief carries itself out, even in the air and earth. pollen on the wind, my name and yours formed in the disconnected breath coiling in our ears for brief rest.

is my grandmother there, wildly turning, dead now five years? is rd? what other ancestors?

i look up again and see coils of rope. many names are written in the threads, i know who cut them and do they think themselves murderers or gods?

yesterday it must have been him riding a slow wind, a puff of pollen among so many i saw, and maybe so many of the collected dead. i thought then, *a solstice snow.*

solstice opens the gates.

*

i have been thinking about oshun recently. how often others focus on the stories of her beauty, her sensual sway like river water, her laugh a tinkling bell. still, her words can burn and her laugh can fill a room at the most inappropriate of times. she is over the top in extravagance and devotion. recently, olorisa reminded me that oshun reminds us of self-sacrifice. there are pataki that describe her transformation into a bird when all the world was burning, who in her rise to the sun, she burns to black, and in her sacrifice she saves the world. her blackness leads to life and fertility and balance, for all. she saves the world; she is beauty in every facet and in how she releases her body's bulk to the aim of love.

and so, with the distance of time, i ask myself, how do i conjure oshun? how do i learn? i think it must come from titi.

is memory the dance of mourning and love that survives long enough to bloom? i love you i love you i love you. i release pain from this love.

*

there is a moment that i never forget. i am at my grandmother's house in the projects in philadelphia. there is the perpetual scent of arroz con gandules in the air as there always seems to be in a boricua house. there are women. titi, my mother, my grandmother. i have this feeling that my grandfather is there, too, but his form is a shadow at vision's edge. merengue plays, and titi says to me, "do you know how to dance merengue? it's just like walking. one. two." and she rises from a patterned couch to dance and then her arms reach down to hold me. though i cannot walk, i dance, her hands keep me in balance.

*

at my grandmother's wake, titi watches me as i watch her. we perform as grief puppets. grief wears us in its theater.

childhood trauma and uncertainty always squelches emotional profundity in me. though earlier in the day, i had laid hours in a fetal position, shaking a bed and a room with weeping, to see me in that moment at the wake – it was if i was watching myself on television – you would have thought that a wake was an entirely mundane place and time. i laughed and made jokes, gossiped with family members, and embraced so many gathered. as in my grandmother's hospital room, nearly 30 people always around her, moving in shifts, we boricua roll deep. her body in the casket, there are hundreds of us, buzzing. the matriarch dead. titi will be the next.

i move with lightness at the wake; it could not possibly be a shattering.

i perform that i have it together. i perform control and joviality. i perform prayerful poise. she performs at the casket, kneels with her hands perfectly clasped, her mother's corpse in front of her. both of us calmly pristine. lying. both of us.

*

at the funeral of my grandmother, she arrives at the church, just a few blocks from my grandmother's last home. my brother is there, my male cousins. they wait for the hearse to arrive so they can carry an empty remnant wrapped in steel.

my other aunt, my father, and uncles gather at the house just those few blocks away to ride in a limousine provided by the funeral parlor. when titi hears this, she calls over and tells them to wait. she goes to the house. she, too, must be wrapped in black steel.

my brother and i grumble, *she said that she wouldn't give a dime to this funeral, but she wants to ride in a limousine.* her smile when she realized she could ride. i remember that as she rushed off. the rare treat that momentarily erases despair.

*

when i saw my grandmother for the last time, i sobbed uncontrollably. i had to be nearly carried away by my brother, my left hand pried from the casket's rim.

at the repast, titi said, "i was wondering when you were going to break. you were holding it together so long. you have to let it out."

i felt bitter at my breaking. i felt bitter that she had seen it, that she was right.

later she said to me and my sister that we have to keep the family together, that this is what our grandmother would have wanted. but how do you stitch shards?

*

at the novena, while helping my cousins and one of my aunts prepare the repast for after the prayers and song, titi comes up behind me, grabs my ass with both hands, lifts it up and shakes. "reinita, you look good with a little weight." she compliments its size and roundness and then she moves on to do something else. my bodily violation nothing. my worth and sovereignty nothing. there is a knife in my hand and suddenly there is someone in front of me who can see my mind empty, how my hand grips so quickly. i don't know who it was who was brave and stepped between us. i only remember that there was a body. that is enough for sense. it is my grandmother's novena. the first day. all of the elders take their seats. i sit on the stairs with my older sister, who is not supposed to be real, woman born out of wedlock, born outside of a priest's damned blessing. we sing and pray from a prayer sheet. it crunches. is that the sugar or some other poison? i am surprised that i know most of the words and melodies from a time i can't clearly remember, when my grandmother's voice would rise until mine joined her in spanish.

later, titi reminds me how we used to rest, my brother and i, on either side of my grandmother when we were very little. and in her story, i remember the rose powder smell, as i nestled under her arm, and she read me the bible. this is a generosity, so i forgive titi the violation of my body.

*

how quickly we forgive when trauma teaches:  to not forgive is to eat your own body.

*

"for someone you don't like, you talk a lot about your aunt," my husband says once.

until then, i had not thought about it. it's true; i've been thinking about why for years.

*

when i was confirmed, i took the name esther, completing the homage to my mother's mother, queen ester, in my name. i asked titi to be my sponsor. first, it was because it was convenient. she only lived a few blocks away and already attended our church. no need for the bureaucracy of catholic paperwork. no need for a letter of upstanding status in the church; she attended the mid-morning sunday mass, nearly always in the same pew, either a few rows back in the right wing or a few rows back from the priest on the nave's right. perhaps this was always about being "to the right" of the altar, if not at the right hand of the father or father priest presiding.

looking back now, i realize i also wanted her to love me, to show love to me in a way that wasn't barbed with expectations for my behavior as a woman, as boricua, as black or not black at all. i wanted her to love me as an extension of pure faith. i wanted the grace to be seen as whole, human, strong.

in the ceremony, i remember her being proud, her face rosy under the lights. the archbishop himself was there to proclaim me confirmed in christ, remade with a new authority in the church with a name i chose for myself. her hand rested on my right shoulder as we reaffirmed baptismal vows, the ones made on my behalf by parents and godparents. this time, my sponsor would say them with me. my voice with hers with god and spirit. i remember feeling hollow, eager for an awe that never came. i knew, even then, that the way she showed love would never be what i wanted or imagined.

if i could teach my younger self, i would tell her to study the ways that she showed love already; that's what i do often now.

as a mother, i look back on another woman who offered me mothering in her own way, who taught me how to be in how i learned to resist. i had to determine my own truth, not follow her or any other.

\*

is this world a madness? i am in the world, of the world. is there a modicum of freedom in this history and want, this swirl of memory around me, so like a parting of air around a blackening bird who will not turn back? is titi the burning sun in this story? or is she one of the spirits in the wind, pushing me higher and higher and higher, pulsing with heat alongside me?

## theophilus underlines emelina's name

confederate worshippers wrote books of _____
lover of god, so wide your eye and stout
your pen, you planted your seed
plantations throughout the carolinas
and across the waters in santo domingo

before the darkness rose
in the bodies you fondled like jewels

you named your children like fronds
maria del carmen, maria antonia, ana maria
blessed mother, their insidious wombs
the records say africans took everything from you
except the eight you seized and stole
to poison saint augustine

from you, a son who named a son
lover of god, too.
the one who sold her and her children.

_____, they say, the family did witchcraft
they learned the ways of black gods
and loved them to scarring
did your people come from the land
sutured by salt

sold for $800
to who would become my uncle machete
down a long river to you
his great-grandson raped god
it can be said no other way
no way to say love
you were solid, a rock
carved to bleed a birthing
a body a passive silver

to whom does one confess
this crime against god
theophilus best translated
as eater of god's flesh

**banned portrait in the maga era:  study says black girls are "less innocent"**

i opened the door and flipped the black lock
of the clear plastic screen with the framing leaves in stained glass
and out into our postage stamp yard

sun-dancing dandelions
yellow heads and the white for wishing
i was making a bouquet for my mother

my father upstairs in the grips of a peace
that comes only after a 16-hour shift in detention
with boys to whom he never showed my picture

it was a boy passing on a tricycle
his mother far behind
that made me rush in fear

back into the house
i wasn't supposed to be seen unguarded
not presentable and perfect

lock
lock
and down

to the basement for more spring bounty
blush tea roses under the tree bursting
cherry to color a world in petal pink

to go there i had to climb a tall shelf
to find the keys
hidden from little hands

three locks one creaky

method of a child's escape? double-handed body
weight hang to turn the key

barefooted i crept out
careful of fallen pointed branch stubs
to snip and slip in my frayed chemise

a satin basket for all the flowers
then back in and lock the three
and up the stairs

to nestle under my father's arm
that smelled
of roasted onion sweat

already the flowers had wilted
i threw them away when i woke
no one noticed the ruin

### give us the pig

after *too obvious,* 1996. david hammons

papi says the pig is dirt
that the whiteness machine wants to feed us refuse
whiteness aches to make us weak

when tito was diagnosed type 1
even insulin had to be swineless
he needed the good human stuff
not what whiteness said was good enough
close enough
because he was human
no refuse
his pancreas heard human
and started acting right

*what kind of puerto rican doesn't eat pork*
my titi vilma would say
the papi-kind
the me-kind
and we black too

still
give us
no choice
give us pig
we will split it
call spirits
claim our human
see the cowrie future
rattle and beat the dance calls
in cleaned bones
and you will see
how strong

our spirits
as they
walk
alongside
our human
cell/ves

**banned portrait in the maga era:  on returning to the united states**

      after *ada rests in places unknown*, 2014. ruby onyinyechi amanze

we wake with dawning, jet lag, the frailty
of our thin forms in and out of time. just days
ago our minds electrified, bursting
beneath fireworks while here plants sun-lazed.

and now we are opposite:  beneath eye
weights, so heavy, though sun seeps its carmine
staining light on a poet's page that i
signal with simple words, *kind of bloodline*.

in twilight, we find a new lust fever
and bemoan our amiable couch-fight while
watching netflix to stay awake, but rest
is not for here or now when the cleavers
descend on black dead and holed; a treason trial
un-started. acquittal surety. i dream loving and depressed.

**digital lynching**

these bodies

breathe

        those trees

thorn hush

        full

hang

        cacophony

necking

        o blossom

tongue black

        murmur pistil

twisted        flutter

smile

        root

police

        bound

still free

**broken haiku:  black god this body**

bless the ovaries
in their lopsided ache, how
they push fatty folds.

*the wheels on the bus*
*go 'round and 'round* through people.

world opens its jaws.

follicle outlines,
"don't you see them? how they grow!"
bombs primed to explode.

acupuncturist,
"his soldiers need to bash heads
to conquer an egg"

after iui,
deep belly burning rises.
pray cherry from ash.

piss over barley
another practice to find
pregnancy stirring

1: could be early.
2: why trust stream mechanics?
3: not enough. thin blood.

spring letter comes. tenured
i want and do not have you.
cut this cord or stay?

academia
i drive hours for vein pricks *(ivf)*
each day they cut my throat *(wtf)*

pictures flood facebook
ultrasound outlines, hidden
thumbs. mother? not me.

i see a friend, green.
know, she's pregnant. a longing
blooms in crevice rust.

in my hidden, two
at the ultrasound, i willed
them found twins
                    polyps

these growing polyps
stood like bright shadow seeds,
                              death
a kind of harvest

                                        black mothers die quick
                                        suddenly appear, full bloom
                                        a hellmouth chews roots

may i be mother?

**banned portrait in the maga era:  afro-latina texts her brother**

~

*why do i keep doing this to myself?*
*so many wypipo, all around me,*
*and the funk and soul music plays on*
*one black man singing to a shaded white crowd:*
*one man's tapping foot, two women dancing*
*all elbows and jut.*
*i can't help counting.*

*i'm the only one who sings the songs of the soul.*

~

eleggua, spirit of crossroads,
san antonio,
saint of lost things. he carries
an old man's stick, tumbles
like a boy, dressed in ragged clothes,
red and black.

*it's the day of pride.*
*stonewall push back against police.*
*rainbows forget brown and black as colors.*
*as people.*
*white isn't there either …*
*is it?*

~

blood currents course around floe sugars:
this must be my brother's claret now,
now that the diabetic devil has returned,
cloaked in ragged white and dancing drunk,
*i was always here*
*calling your name.*

⁓

in philadelphia, i imagine melting, too,
earthen body become ice,
his sweat glistens the skin to diamonds.
tito reads my texts, laughs.
*i don't what it is to not be the only.* wry.
he gives me his password for *game of thrones.*
is winter still coming or is it here? i forget.


⁓

i left all the handkerchiefs i bought
to sop my weeping, back
in my ruin-rising house.


⁓

*somewhere there is a black child*
*holding a hand to a candle*
*to see a red tide course*
*around bone spindles,*
*forgetting the burn*
*to witness their own thin skin*
*peeled away to true.*

augment

**prophet sing** *the whole world*

i dance muscle atrophy to diagram
        i have it all *the whole world* in my hands
i can nose out the mirror truth
        cartwheel quick through dermis into comet-spray with one touch
cosmos blueprints through body pathways a black divine in the dna
        *i know i know*        persona cartographer sidling up in mink and a cadillac
time be time but knows no time
        world be out but close as a thumbprint coil
prick *the whole world*     don't you want to sing
        don't you want to bang the bells        chime a look ahead and here comes
you can't catch me     i am already in you
        sometimes i dream myself *matrix neo*
cool prophet        but no savior   no saving        string tendon as harp
        play the texture to skip like a child on three popsicles
transmit the boxing balance life        the depth
        be rex-glorious *the whole world*   don't you want it too
this unfrozen light        the dust dance
        brutally tussle back into a new celestial form

**consolation of mothers**

    *for beata mariana de jesús mejía mejía* and her child

i offer this. this is the suffering.
before a fire crown splits in a ring,
your body nests — ova within ova within ova, all possibilities
and promise of an eye fleck that remains yours –
you are changed.
you will never stop being mother. never stop distilling ocean
water for sweet or carrying the weight of child.

in this swell and expanding oscillation of waddle,
i learned this lesson and can conjure
no matter the distance or years,
both in their reaching shadows,
i will always know the press of my child's foot,
the imprint on innards to bleeding,
the path of my organs permanently transmuted.

at the border, your son is torn from your back
that carried him from his father's beaten erasure,
desiccation, all the vulnerabilities of travel
without country among the bloody-mouthed.
in this place of freedom, you lose your son to chain links,
his easy laugh and tinkling bell voice.
after weeks, you find the right number to call,
find his timbre changed, heavy with *something happened*.
he is not the boy who never touched ground.
he is a child spiked through with american steel,
his throat-song ground to tinny clink.

i'm supposed to console you.
there is no solace
in the slow flay, the violent stripping
of child from mother.

## hypatia teaches that they come for the women who know

serapis this meteor pock  bleeds a fire
you stitch   how this pink colors into earth
hair prickles slow          the mob peels my virtue
            patient in torture          twist smiles and silver rings
serapis pray me daughter again

was it my skin that called their cutting oyster shells
αιχμηρός [i]                    plane thin to papyrus-tone flesh
                    soak the flap for three days                    layered resurrection
i die for vellum carved to my voice

to know the law is to write
on still throbbing tendon

*father*                                roof tiles for sheaves
and all my letters swirl me numb

what does a girl know of suffering
never felt her brown skin scroll unspooled for flick-flame eyes
not even a spit-rain reprieve

animals

serapis see here
years i labored with why          chisels on river-worn stone

alexandria          law          sharp teething

i never wanted my animal to rule
rune      inkcurve        chiparchive          stainheal          mage

-----

[i] pronounced aichmirós, meaning sharp in greek

someone is dead          so many someones          start a library to know

or just be a woman who speaks

**in the beginning**

it's in the sheen, still cosmic shine and glitter, over your cheeks and forehead as you sucked on your two fingers, index and middle, in the time when most babies would be sleeping. that external gleam, a mica dermis splatter — always made me recall how you came to me in a dream, angelic riding on the force of an earthquake to tell me your name, tell me you were in my cavity, central, the day before the blood tests confirmed that i was pregnant. that shine over the cream of your skin made a quilt of light and memory, too, of how i had a reiki healer to maneuver my energies in the days before you broke the seals of me in so much water, how she said, wafting an eagle's feather, that she could sense an angelic presence over me. yes, you were there, all around me, without and within. an elemental magic.

in the times immediately after your birth, as i wrote minute reflections on social media of this motherescence, this ascendency into a new identity, that of the mother and writer and academic and partner in parenting and life, i used the hashtag — #thisisthebeginningofanessay — to organize, to be able to easily look back to this becoming of me and me in relationship to you.

this is how we began, celestial, embodied spellwork, light-filled.

**behind my eyes, i dance our becoming**

dusk skirt          still shining with brightest star-gods
          or are those digable planets          orb circles like me on pointe
tutu tulle                    full flair                    twinkle wild in traveling spot
          tombée, pas de bourrée, glissade, jeté, susu
triumph singularity        sprig lean rod straight                body caught
          dull sounds the feet                like eyelashes flutter in flirt
and down one leg and to the back                grace brush
          wave the lantern of hand                *come home querida    crash*
*right here at the marked place*        no need for eyes to search masking tape x
          search putter-putter heart low in the west                marked sweep in frame
there's an audience just beyond the light rim                rim shot smarting  unmoving still
          in curve and cushion                weave from earth          numberless hands in thread up and wave
an audience without breath beyond        a mosh pit hot in galactic ore
          crash the stars with the tease sequins in quick
                                        what was that constellation name?

**how body unhinges to birth**

serpent

stone coil

gilded in plume

vibrato o captured

aniconic reminder

river god hold!

headless dust swirl

voice fount

light the dance

exhale and flame


lightening      quiver beneath skin

root descends within      a lake before rupture

no reckoning for start      breakthrough!

chartless waters      shapeshifting

fire is a ring to all beginnings      fish to mewling mouth

### a child witnesses his birth

*mother said we are not supposed to live forever.*

*mother said women open the dead gates*

*mother said we make the body brave. we carry, but we are supposed to go, too.*

*mother said all vessels break. atoms collide and here birth new spheres, a pulsar set in a chest.*

*mother said make way and return and to water be water.*

*mother said the child. mother said* i will give him life, not my loss.

*mother said come come come.*

                                                     *i turn and set my head to light.*

                           *hushing darkness through reddening to a golden burn.*

                                    *angel, kiss my left eyelid. stork, release this neck.*

*the child pushes root-nest. the midwife brushes his hair.*

*the child bathes in mother. rush out spirit cordage for push.*

                                                   *she says a name.*

                                                      *it is my name.*

                                                     *bloody and firmed.*

 *mother says light light.*

*mothers says feed.*

                                                     *god, oh god. this body.*

**potter**

sometimes my baby's weird smile unsettles. it's like he's still figuring out how to fix his look-putty into a smile and gauge how others react to him, like he's molding himself in front of the eye for the gaze he anticipates. he has been here before. there are these moments he totally gets it, when he knows what he knows and can fix the face of him. the light just breaks through what one might call a countenance, because it must be noted as that elegant even, and perhaps because of the toothless and gummy twists, i wonder at how i birthed this being, so full of joy yet tinged with an ochre ache.

**whole human purpose**

a self: today i got to be puerto rican, african american, and taino on an official government form for my son's birth certificate. my identities had official categories. all my life i've been fighting boxes and writing in my identities on lines. in high school, i was as a different ethnicity every year because i listed them all and someone else chose, most likely based on a quota they wanted to fill. someone fought to be recognized, particularly as taino, and here in berkeley there was a system that saw a people. back to singing protest songs as lullabies. what doors will my children open for others?

just 8 days after he was born, nia wilson. sing again. how with a cut throat? sing still. so many names. so many mothers moaning into harmony. god, why can't we sing more life? if not in the bones' brunt, sing a spark. ash makes fertile, too.

**the only color**

*verde, verde, verde* every color is *verde*
and i think on federico garcía lorca,
how i read this poem to him, days old,
his whole body less than six pounds on my chest
and now he stands a wild octopus boy
on a chair reaching for the markers.
*verde, verde* he says, though the uncapped tool
marks page to orange and his father says,
he knows what the best color is.
i say, *naranja o anaranjado, he has to know his colors*
and go into a diatribe about school,
not being behind. it is not about school.

he is my son and so the box waits:
a check mark of abuses woven into his identity.
will he ever be able to just be the creative child
who says *verde, verde, verde* for all the colors,
glorified for how his mind stretches divergent?
my husband does not know that the box
can be a casket and each day
we must fight for it not to be.

ahmaud ran on a street lined with green leaves.
lorca wrote a poem. they shot him, too,
so bright. i just want my son
to know his colors and live.

### on changing my son

after *a city with a river running through it*. ficre ghebreyesus


i am the one who sees olive fields plump their pitted fruits in the green of my son's eyes        the mottled iris
in radiant hickory        a quorum of trees split in their canopy song        this skin   here is the painter's palette an
overlay        city map fashioned in sun flecks        when nude he splays himself unashamed
his being learning being through touch        joy        he has never known shame        my life was ever preparing to
witness freedom        the squirm        *be hummingbird   be boy*        *be bee        be all the natural things*  look
there conch swirls at the edge like those on his thumb   each coil an inherited story  and stories to come  his
body a city within cities of bodies        i never knew this would happen when i refused to play with dolls
when i ripped their heads off        fastened them wild screeching beasts mounted on my brother's remote control
cars        the new harpies all raw warrior defiant        this boy now whose first sound heard was his sweet
name   i knew this        always standing on the threshold to cross a border whose key was not a fist        i am
changed        he is changed   *abre la boca drink*        there is no salt in this land        no arid dust   *only
milk*

**a time magic**

for my son


i am writing you a new spell that uncoils from the spell of your making       silver   filament   thread   that carried your glimmer to lining rest   chosen and made   frozen and unfrozen,  carried and placed by a needle measured in microns       womb a fabric pinprick              i write you a spell that in print will gild the ways possible         in speech will take shape in your bone set and viscosities       i watch you in baby form asleep beneath stripes of white and black          you are firelight cast free   i write you the spell of freedom in water ice        thought grooved into page       i write you angelic sheen that you carry on your cheeks still in this sixth month           ever after      the stroller channels gravel in winter's quiet park   as i tap keys   my bare feet on white marble while you sleep in crib      your papá snores his lullaby       only the dead know whose mouth first formed it   tide in you ripples out then back again       vulnerability in reverb        to birth you i consulted a reiki healer          i filled my house with orange roses   held rose quartz        offered my points to an acupuncturist's needles so many other healers        chanted *heal* within my own mind      offered vortexes swirling within me       a fixed softness to welcome        you who are a sign of water born between luck of 16 and unluck of 17         this spell the first work of your tempo   may you see generations     be free be free be free

**dismemberment**

horror also known as nightmare: my child dies in rising flood waters in puerto rico. i knew him by his onesie. i was holding on to the edge of a levee i had pulled myself onto in the flood while i watched him carried off by receding waters.

this was followed by a nightmare in which my father lost his right arm above the elbow after an accident with church pews at my grandmother's grave site. it seems my mother had commissioned a painted concrete marker to extend from the gravestone. the artists were there, finishing the first day of their work. it was a scene of the annunciation, the blessed mother's substantiate making itself dust as it rises into the heavens, eternal. beautiful. as they left, we noticed a funeral nearby, and the attendants had brought church pews and set them on other graves for people to sit while grieving someone being buried. my father was upset to find one so close to my grandmother's gravesite, one that might mar the art. there was a battle over pews, my father moving them away and the attendants moving them back until eventually my father fell in such a way that the bone of his upper arm snapped and protruded from his arm. i made a poor tourniquet and because an ambulance would not come to a graveyard in this dream, my mother, brother, husband and i (i think baby was in this dream too, but as an empty bassinet) sped down the highway to find help. it all ended with finding an ambulance down a dark road in what seemed to me to be northeast philly near my uncle's neighborhood. a nurse removed the tourniquet of my deliriously calm father to a torrent of blood. his arm was amputated and cauterized with hot copper (i still have the oddest details).

when i woke up to go to the bathroom, i found the furnace not working. i checked the baby's temperature and his hands were cold. the rest was fine, but as i was holding and feeding him, i felt my spirit still pulsing in the nightmare. the unsettledness of the dreams came back. in fact, it never left.

**freedom dreaming is a symphony**

most beautiful:  a friend, sensing i was down and ill, orchestrated a four-part harmony song with
a theater company she led that praised what i had done for others and for her. a measure here for
affirmations and a measure here for a meal. a measure here for being birth plan ready. another measure
for  passion flower blooms bundled to go after tea. the score was embroidered on fabric that unfolded
from the stand. the song ended with a chorus on freedom and finding liberation. together. how we
worship in one another's joy and healing. it was so beautiful. i woke up crying.

**mother sexed**

desire threads itself up the veins of my left leg, a fertile pain that pushes into groin pulse. my animal moans i catch in my throat, control my breath, my pant, a small tantric practice, energy pull and swell. how the body blushes with heat. i am a rippling pool of remembrance. beneath the folds of the maternal body i feel my youth as a dancer, lithe and hard. two bodies in one memory. both sexed and sexy. it is not my husband's voice that sets to fire, nor a long fuzzied and faded recollection of forever sepia lover. it is mine this rise to orgasm, the sharp smell of ozone in my nostrils. electric. i am alone, without the child who is my sweetest daily delight or the partner who elicits giggles and thrills. i am alone, this night in self-adoration. i coast a choppy wave, still as the abandoned surfboard, the dance, the ride without rider.

**beyond hardware**

i peruse paint samples to learn what shade names you. a blend of calumet cream and ivory and at your cheek blush rose, but i didn't need a color chart for that. at six months you have lost the shimmer that teens buy cheap or steal in their first transgressions, but for a time, there it was, free, this fleeting mica fleck, as if you were still dipped in celestial, all known and unknown elements you rode to my pulsing womb. all these months, i watched the star dust fade, the cosmic hold loosening to terra firma. and now, you are dressed in a soft blue onesie with little ears. what animal does capitalism say that you are? *your little one is safe and warm and held and ours*, it seems to say. stupid symbols, charts, and systems. stupid the act of reaching for a fixation. in my womb, i felt a girl and then at 10 weeks when your sex organs formed, a boy. now sometimes i forget the sex i bore and use pronouns that are mine for you. shake loose of it all. i never asked you to tell me your name; you told me at your being start. all i know is that i bore you. nursed you as i was able. only you can name you. i know nothing else.

**liquid gold and otherwise**

i miss having my own brain sometimes. sometimes he does these private, cheeky little smiles that are so fleeting, catching them a wonky magic, a giggle delight, and suddenly i'm not too worried about to-do lists, parchment rolls of unfinished tasks in my mind. babies are magicians like that.

today, i pumped five times for less than 10 ml of liquid gold. in the smallest bottle we have, it doesn't even get to the first mark.

i do not cry. cut his tongue and bleed from the nipple to feed him. these the mechanics to putter along.

**pass the dark and stormy**

how the liquor lacquers my tongue slick
for a moment
i am joyous

where is my baby?

at the bottom
of a glass
no
over an ocean
my laughter
effervescent bubbles

in a corner
of my mind
my parents cluck their tongues
*is this why you left him*
*with his father?*
*a baby far from mother withers*
or some guilt that thuds
in a pool i do not swim.

i am drunk
in an airport
a moment while planes land
guided by flags and flashing light
while baby sleeps sound
loved close and distant
and this is also
a mothering
so true
it bleeds.
see it
there?

**augmented**

**atrial septal defect or we must leave this country before my son turns 12**

~

sometimes i fear the casket shroud
will emerge from my own shadow
to greet me smiling with my son's teeth.

this country is such a cruel winter
to black boys singing their spirits from dread; it hangs
their songs to clink on snow covered boughs.

my sister's son died & she wore white,
only two months, his heart already broken
in its making. with tamir & ayana & honestie,

black babies in a pandemic of guns & crowns,
i whisper to myself his new name: prophet.
call her grief pure.

a natural end and still a butchering.
sometimes i see him somersaulting in her wake.
& sometimes i fear how my still
new name, *mamma*,
might be written in soot on snow.

~

his twin is 8 now. their sister is 2,
continuum of earth.
color codes:
field of gleeful browns.
my son is black & he is parchment in cream.

this northern city has grime and glint
in its racism.

my boy's buttermilk
may save their black
though he is black.
it may not save anyone at all.

am i raising a boy
or what a surgeon might call
vulnus sclopetarium or
slab with a child.

~

it was me who held his twin sister's
twisting hands to his before curtains were drawn.
it was me who carried her screaming
from the room to a hospital labyrinth.

~

by the time i was 8, i could break a jaw into bone spires. i learned to handle a knife in philadelphia:
slice quick to splatter an invitation to rubber gloves. i swore they would find me still deadly in shaking
sheen if ever a fool would. since my boy was six weeks old, i have folded his hands to combination.
jab, jab, cross. block to hide the smile i want to save, even when he was gum & dribble. an elder in a
newborn's bib.

in germany, three days it took
to leave the serrated honing behind.
i felt safer in a place of dead crematoriums
than my own country.

~

if my boy falls to metal, unnatural, shard me up, abyss cut water to darkness. if a building stand, it is a
lie. a forest of names for empty-eyed women the only real. also, real: this country will kill you if you're
not looking and even if you are.

mother my god? she asked me
mother? my god.
my god.

**we never talk about this: chemical pregnancy**

> after "solitary boat" by ficre ghebreyesus with chorus from "stay" by carol maillard of sweet
> honey in the rock

*the clock on the wall*
*says it's time to go*

in the dream knowledge pounced
and i felt i was pregnant again
woke from sleep and felt the hard secret nut
the uterus in its first swell
just before sleep i had seen a shadow dog
in the corner between desk and television
i worried it had appeared to mouth your brother's essence and steal it away
i prayed over him
called on his angels and my grandmother as mine for protection
did it come for you instead?

*the clock on the wall*
*says it's time to go*

days later when i learned you were no longer in me
flesh expelled in a blood tinged webbing of mucus
how the body shows a spoiled seed's end long before the fruit
i saw a painting of a lone boat in a dark sea
there were no people
had they already drowned in their migration across troubled waters
with only the tubing's garish yellow remaining
orbs abandoned to the latest hours
bridge lights lit far off

you who were a being of water and flesh and gold and wind
a breath slip, gone before a name could fix you,
i imagined you swayed in the boat
then a twisted seaweed pat in the tumble of invisible waves

then a pebble that falls too fast to be carried

you were more than a number on a test i begged the doctor to give me
regarded again as insane for knowing my own meat
and when she saw the proof said miracles do happen
as if the miracle was the numbers
my sanity a miracle
as if you were passively placed and not already animate with your lessons to teach
in form and unforming
as if

i ponder brush strokes
it may take me a lifetime to understand
someday i will seek you beyond my eye's sight
i will give you this poem
i will ask your name

i feel the light around me
you are in that light
on gilded water

*the clock on the wall*

**hover**

above us there are no helicopters
not like when the wind
smelled like california soot
and every hour sirens wove
their hair into ours and sung
names to enchant cacophony
*say their names* and we were home
your sister newborn in my arms
protecting her life a protest

weeks before, each time a plane
scored the berkeley sky in white
you would point up
say *mamma* because i am always
in the sky even when my skin
burns in the sun next to yours
how my eyes leak with storms
you cannot yet name
we stand in unhinged weather

there are no helicopters today
you bang on a wheelbarrow
with dried bamboo stalks as drum sticks
and lift your toddler throat up to shout
*'cotto*! over and over again
a screamo chorus
lyrics perfectly formed to your ears
i nod only yes
and keep beat

at the people's park
marchers assemble
with banners of *i can't breathe*

san pablo, i can hear
the horns of a car parade
inside the mourners shout behind masks
from open windows
while a virus flies around us all
pandemic in crown
and white


surrounded by fences
i can keep you safe
and breathing
until i can't
every door has the threat of splinter

there are no helicopters today
'*cotto* you yell

somewhere they descend
somewhere a body hangs
halfway between metal and earth

## 21 caskets in an infinity line

*at the head of the line, that casket, belongs to my wife's mother. that's a matriarch there, my children's grandmother there, and so many more behind her.* we are at a funeral. the poet speaks in the dream. all the pallbearers are black men in crisp suits with white gloved hands. they slide the caskets, black and polished to shine, one after another down a church aisle. 21. someone in that line is one of mine, a man i fantasized could hold me when i was still girl trying to be someone such a man could see. i know i know many more. those who mourn in person wear their masks and spread their bodies across the church. there are screens that unfold their wailing faces. mechanized masks that should short for all the water and salt in the air. when i wake, i say, *this is how i process the grief.* the remembrances of longed for intimacy. the passage of years and now he's gone and so is she and they and oh so many. virus, bullet, knee, rope. eventually we are all calcium white. the baby i carry i thought would split me open early, eager to be in this world, but now, i feel her fingers at the gate, how they press to stitch me closed. the womb is a safer dance than blossoms and birth is just another path to die drowning in your own undulating tissue.

**person of interest**

it does not matter
how many times
i say
my body is not a threat
how many times
the tests come back negative
i am always a person of interest
suspect
even in birthing a child
who could be a
virus criminal
like me
corona a crown
we could share

### for a daughter on the n$^{th}$ day of self-isolation

your brother cries in the dawning of each day,
wrested by body from dream delight
into the routines. he takes the milk.
he asks for "baby," which is short
for a television program he loves
because it teaches how to communicate in asl,
how to bridge the chasm with we giant
between words we know & he invents.
i tell him that he is the "baby"
& that there is a baby, too, within me.
sometimes, he lifts my dress or shirt
& sticks his finger into my belly button
or tries to lodge a magnet there
as if to touch your hand,
as if to call you out,
as if to prove that he knows you are there.

in my walk from bed to kitchen,
your papá already there with bottle in hand,
your name emerged as if it had always been there,
aurélia, the name of the road to genova,
the home of your grandmother's people,
as much a road as it is a journey
for a people who bleed the sea.

we make our home a ship without sails.
hospitals now say a pregnant mother with covid-19
will have a c-section
will be separated from the newborn
for up to 14 days
will birth alone
& so i gird myself in loneliness
to protect us both from separation,

a kind of early death
when the first hours call for clinging,
the first suck of your mouth at my breast,
the first coos of my mouth to your ear.
*this is your name. we crossed a rough sea*
*together.*
*here we are,*
*daughter,*
*whole & ever entangled,*
*whole & separate*
*in light & breath & blood.*

i try not to fear the devil outside.

**suspect**

in the isolation room, there are dirt spots on the floor. in laboring, as the contraction waves rise to peak pain and then taper, i focus on dirt. i am riding a wave above the soiling. the child washes me over in hot spray. my skin sheens over in glow. a nurse says, *you are so strong* and *you are doing so well.* her affirmations are cracked glass on a see-through bridge; i do not trust. how can i when i cannot see her lips, her face, beneath the blue mask? i, too, am masked. it's a dirty exchange. i think in expletives. i try to return to the wave. i ask for a heating pad. they will never bring it. my touch is contagion, suspected contagion. i am guilty until proven innocent. a fever is pandemic. a black body is pandemic. a fever is not a possible sign of labor, though i am laboring. the child pushes blood through the gate, announces herself. the heft takes over. the doctor says, "do whatever your body tells you." as if i could stop her entrance on this human water, the fertile spark of me a path into an isolation filled with people. i focus on the spots and their erasure. mine.

**mother fear**

there are birds on the water
feather flight and swirling vortex

you would know her name if you could sing
like the nightingale or swift with their tales

nanostructurally composed to shine
as they set down and alight

they conjure in this internal world
set to their spinning by a glint syringe

science the magician of creation
all worlds crumble and crash

this one in a dilated door
labor has its own clock unless a doctor ordains

a being just a murmuration of swallows
or a murder under a bloody sheet

**thoth become woman in the mirror**

*law 127: "if any one 'point the finger' at a sister of a god or the wife of any one, and can not prove it, this man shall be taken before the judges and his brow shall be marked."*
code of hammurabi

i watch her with my blue-film eye
skimmed thin to oracle her future

watch the moon open her face
calculate her preening in weather
today : beneath the clouds a lovesick waltz
tomorrow : gaslight apocalypse

how many times has the law told a woman
your name is wound that should gape

how many times has a doctor told a woman
your body is a knob for my turning

i could write the numbers
on a mountain made of glass
and need to form more from all time's sands

i see spirit worms rippling beneath our skin
mambo frenzy     twist-twine gourd rattle shake

she dreams in pointed fingers

the flayers will always come

better to be a moon pocked
it is still a heavenly body

**eden had four rivers**

after the birth and the afterbirth, the midwife lifts the placenta to show how from womb we are all elemental, *beloved,* succored from a veiny tree. the assigned boy child was easy. *querido querida querides* , we took the organ, *of our lineage,* a treasured gift, *of our waters and roots,* iced and carried in a bloody plastic bag, *a budding,* and contributed its last work to fig. after the assigned girlchild, *wherever you go from around to within,* we had to steal what they wanted to study. mother as creature made possible pathology. we brought a cooler and guarded it. peaches rise now in a garden that feeds other mouths. *breath ancestor los ancestros que todavía respiran están respirando sus canciones* trees rose and the roots talked to one another. all creatures listened and knew one language. they moved like water, *we see you,* adapting to one another. and in the water, *we be you,* that fed the water and trees and all living things, *you be we,* there was wisdom and memory passed on. *areyto to atabey remembered in stone* on a metal tray, *strength current wherever there is water and earth,* a deliverer holds up a blood tree, roots the bridge between death and life and dream, *fleshy eden,* listen to the voices still whispering there before the clot. *springtime in mewl and eyelash flutter. our and your own yes.*

## hole

after my first, they said,
*track marks*
as in
he came so fast he left
*track marks*. not skid.

within a few weeks
i stopped bleeding
tarred to smooth highway
clean black in rain
skid or addict lane?

after my second, they said
*a small tear*
*stitch or silver nitrate*
and i chose the chemical
it didn't burn
a newborn a kind a balm

weeks again
a highway again
this time pitted and raw
*i know exactly where the tear was*
pandemic
no one will examine me
a body is always contagion
the midwife gives me
a recommendation for a doctor
who will pat my hand
*there there*
*there's no pain now, right?*
and also not examine the damned spot

the first time
it is a physical therapist
amazed at ambulatory dysfunction
*you have a wound*
*very slight*
*you need more silver nitrate to heal the skin*
*that's why you have such pain*

and then three more weeks to be seen
an appointment almost canceled
i beg to tears over a tear
and when i arrive, my medical records
are perused
*there there*
she looks hesitantly
sees a wound
at touch bleeds a river
on a q-tip
*you still have a tear*
*the wound isn't healing*
*we can try this again*
*but if it doesn't work*
*we will have to revise it*
which means cut a skin sliver
wider and deep
while i dream my death
and sew me tight
like before
a first time

when i tell my husband,
he mourns
the loss of my limbs
in sex

when i left the doctor,
*nice to meet you*
*thanks for burning me*
*see you soon*

**sequence**

first baby.

help. i am pinned beneath a sleeping baby. i dare not move. cute little baby hair tickles my chin. glorious torture. i have things i'd like to do that my thumb and iphone are not capable of doing effectively.

today i described myself to my mother as a cow academic without the academic. my son shows me his full frustrated self when he's up for play and social time with others and responds to me with desperation as food source. i am not a thinking human; i am a blinking animal with leaking breasts. i enter a room and all amazement he offers to my husband, mother, anyone, shifts to pursed lips ready for a latch. i'd heard of this dehumanization from other mothers but figured it might take a while. by two weeks, he was not entertained by play or politicizing of baby via protest slogans in baby friendly tones. my son smells or hears my voice and thinks food.

second baby.

long emails come when the children are sleeping, when i have time to put action items at the top of the email and document the supporting logic at the bottom. short emails when i am using one thumb and rocking a baby in the dark.

in the first days, we set a nursery/guest bedroom up in our dining room. there is my daughter's bassinet, her smaller co-sleeping one i keep on the bed or take into the garden when she is a few weeks old. when she mewls, i give her the knock out juice, which i know is only, at most, a few drops of breastmilk. she rests a while and then always cries for more. outside there are occasionally protest parades and horns. with her in my arms, we breathe together in alexis pauline gumbs' black feminist breathing chorus. breathing freedom, breathing our flourishing, breathing the possibility and reality of our joy. how i love her and my "muah schmack" boy who blows me a kiss each time he passes the small and simple coocoo. i hold her weight on me, still, until we both mix little puddles of sweat. sometimes i rock, going everywhere in my mind and nowhere at all. we are all animals. every one.

## charon, undertaker for our blackest beloveds

(what to do
with bodies
thin-skinned fruit split
for too much too little

(slice them thin
bone spires

(in sky extended hands
curl finger shards
around sapling roots
cover deep
whispers

(beneath soil ripples
a twining
above silence come
sacred down

(i listen
know their names
a while

(storm claps
in tree shivers
fear that propels
bullet burns
so many sacks

(an empty rehearsal
no one to direct
and soothe
a lifeless death

a deathful life

(i cannot hitch
a seed and soul
to every waste

(call me a new name
one that exhales
myrrh

**to the doctor i say i might be perimenopausal and am prescribed an inhaler**

the first stains were rusty tracks on cotton white. i hid my dying and went on with days. my mother did the laundry and knew and did not say. there was no celebration circle or moon party; i got a blue covered book from the library  i would have to return. we did not talk about what made a woman flesh.

after my son's birth, i was all blood and wound healing, globule eggs i birthed, how they would split in a spray a tissue. a bed, a scene for my maiden murder. this is how a woman becomes a mother, i thought, the massacre of all those other selves visceral in stain. i threw away the sheets i could not wash clean.

i read that after my womb sutured itself i might enjoy up to a year bloodless while feeding him my milk, but no. a month and i was a flood, for the first time of my life painless, a slick shedding. i walked tall and happy. just days of happening that led to not.

and with my daughter, the same. twice. pain not a part of the becoming as an invitation to another becoming. and then

stop. blood. milk.

six months of invitation to sweet rivers, lover dive and discover. an entangled free delight. there has been no red.

i remember wanting a child, sweaty nights.

i ached for lust, received
more desire for supernatural television than a body.

i confess
the gods shook me barren, a surgical till my only hope for life.

there is a ghost i named
who called me in silence and mucus

now i am bloodless.

massacre complete. i see crone in mirrors.

am i ugly, darling, in this wake for the corpse of my girlhood?

or free.

yes, i hold all the tongues of past and possibility.

breathe deep. a breath thick with clots.

**our daughter is born two days after george floyd called out to his dead mother or he says he sees this is racism**

to witness how different
our care by doctors
knows this is racism
and my proximity
to whiteness may keep
me and our child alive

my blood condemns us
in birthing continues
may my name in her mouth
never be said in fear
never *mama, they kill me*
our ancestors again
and all the possibilities
*mama, i'm through*
pop

**at aiden's funeral, ever 58 days old, who would have just started school**

*to the babe and my two sisters/fellow godmothers*

air an aria,
bird rib.
                    *won't it now?!*
                                   *halle-ah*
*cigar? toss it in a can. it is so tragic.*
                    *murder for a jar of red rum.*
                                   *won't lovers revolt now?*


we few
we panic in a pew.
*do geese see god?*


rats live on no evil star,
name no one man
deified.
dogma in my hymn:  i am god.


sagas


dogma in my hymn:  i am god.
deified
name. no. one man.
rats. live on no evil. star,
do geese see god?
we panic. in a pew,
we few
murder for a jar of red. rum?
won't lovers revolt now?
cigar. toss it in a can. it is so tragic,
                                   *halle-ah*
          *won't it now?!*
bird rib
air. an aria.

**what we lose in the fire a blown tire makes us see**

the slight glimmer of wedding dress beading
once slicked down by nervous palms before the aisle

the detritus of childhood, her last baby tooth
so recently shook in a pink fairy box

the long unplayed cello that must have sounded out
its own urging to the fire that licked it to char

all the books, the blessed books
the devastation of libraries that burn

our tenderest treasures, a mandala
prayer written in gold

all the flecks of us layered in disparate places
the hair balls crevice-resting

we burned there though we were not there
or perhaps we were and

only high flying birds could intuit our story
as they flew in circles cinder-blinded until they fell

for the trees are tinder
and the earth grays over

above a death mare's mane blocks the sun
searing still in orange glow

how terrible the psychedelic colors at sunset
how terrible the smoldering

and still we did not lose our eyes
seeing the blaze for wonder

what was and what might be

**decay**

child, i am old
and have learned so many rules
of what and how to taste,
how manufactured foam
on a lightly poached egg
refines the tongue
while sea sputum
twists it to poison, they say,
and though i know gold
clogs the intestines to stillness
and cements there
even in tiny flecks,
their glitter going down
is supposed to be
a culinary delicacy
better than the sun's
momentary grace
on studded palate.

child, what would you teach me about gluttony?

tell me about this second meal,
so soon after the grit of the sandbox
and just before the dessert of your own spit
as you suck your fingers.

querida, describe how death ribbons in your mouth,
how the fall leaves offer you a new pucker
a distinct scrunch to your face.
is this how your first wrinkle of consternation forms?

when i die, will the leaves i eat
taste like these i disparage now

thinking them less fine
on a menu you sample of garden?

**augmented reality**

**earthly abundance divine embodied** *(art from fele)*

**soundtrack**

don't touch my hair. **at the purchaser's option**. [so] weary. **aguanile.** oya, **this is america**. bad, bad news. **drone bomb me** running up that hill. **cranes in the sky.** sincerely, jane. **warrior heart** [sing the] song of the agitators. **wayfaring stranger,** ain't gotta worry child. i wanna be like you. **time after time,** valé **para ochun.** preach **freedom,** i am her. **black gold** [&] songbird [&] **higher vibe** [&] true colors

and we stay in song and dance and fiercely loving this god who is such a mother

https://tidal.com/browse/playlist/d8d229fb-077c-4e69-98f9-ea5d2b6daf53
http://bit.ly/blackgodmother

# acknowledgements

the author gratefully acknowledges the following publications that offered a home to the following poems in various iterations:

banned portrait in the maga era:  afro-latina texts her brother, *queen mob's teahouse*
banned portrait in the maga era:  black god this body, *santa clara review*
banned portrait in the maga era:  consolation of mothers, *queen mob's teahouse*
banned portrait in the maga era:  on returning to the united states, *kore press*
banned portrait in the maga era:  study says black girls are less innocent, *jung journal* and *poetry and parks/quiet lightning anthology 2017*
beyond hardware, *green mountains review* and *Até Mais/Until More: An Anthology of Latinx Futurisms*
black prophet of extinct, lonely, and killer trees, *vitriol*
a child witnesses his birth, *poetry and parks/quiet lightning anthology 2017*
chiron, undertaker for our blackest beloveds, *vitriol* and *remembering the days that breathed pink* anthology
from the adyton, *studio one anthology*
give us the pig, *packinghouse review*
hole, *la libreta*
hope of the ancestral and unbodied, *vitriol* and *poetry and parks/quiet lightning anthology 2017* and *furious flower: seeding the future of african american poetry* anthology
hover, *SWIMM daily*
mother sexed, *580 split*
nearly 5000, *kweli*
on changing my son, *a dozen nothing*
the only color, *VIDA*
pass the dark and stormy, *580 split*
testimonio, *Smithsonian Day of the Dead celebration 2021*
thoth become woman:  codice signifier, *anthro/poetics*
to the doctor i say i might be perimenopausal and am prescribed an inhaler, *la libreta*
we never talk about this:  chemical pregnancy:  *the long devotion: poets writing motherhood* anthology
what we lose in the fire a blown tire makes us see, *digital lit garden* and *furious flower: seeding the future of african american poetry* anthology

this collection was also nurtured in the following communities: alley cat books residency; the poetry incubator in chicago; the hackermoms community; the guest house artist residency in cork, ireland; the sf writers grotto, salmon bookshop artist residency of ennistymon, ireland; the saint mary's college of california mfa in creative writing program; the afro-surreal writers workshop; the museum of the african diaspora poet-in-residence program; the berkeley art museum and pacific film archive reading series; the speakeasy project writing community; la tertulia boricua; the acentos review and the acentos community; cantomundo; macondo; cave canem; the carolina african american writers collective; furious flower; studio one; the bay area writing community; the community of writers; voices of our nations arts (vona); the ó bhéal writing community; the cork arts community; and so many who have fostered my work. i give thanks, too, to cedric tillman, and tongo eisen-martin who specifically gave sharp eyes to this book.

**Raina J. León**, PhD is Black, Afro-Boricua, and from Philadelphia (Lenni Lenape ancestral lands). She is a mother, daughter, sister, madrina, comadre, partner, poet, writer, and teacher educator. She believes in collective action and community work, the profound power of holding space for the telling of our stories, and the liberatory practice of humanizing education. She seeks out communities of care and craft and is a member of the Carolina African American Writers Collective, Cave Canem, CantoMundo, Macondo. She is the author of *Canticle of Idols*, *Boogeyman Dawn*, *sombra : (dis)locate*, and the chapbooks *profeta without refuge* and *Areyto to Atabey: Essays on the Mother(ing) Self*. She publishes across forms in visual art, poetry, nonfiction, fiction, and scholarly work. She has received fellowships and residencies with the Obsidian Foundation, Community of Writers, Montana Artists Refuge, Macdowell, Kimmel Harding Nelson Center for the Arts, Vermont Studio Center, the Tyrone Guthrie Center in Annamaghkerrig, Ireland and Ragdale, among others. She is a founding editor of *The Acentos Review*, an online quarterly, international journal devoted to the promotion and publication of Latinx arts. She educates our present and future agitators/educators as a full professor of education at Saint Mary's College of California, only the third Black person (all Black women) and the first Afro-Latina to achieve that rank there. She is additionally a digital archivist, emerging visual artist, writing coach, and curriculum developer.

"There's a ship
The Black Freighter
With a skull on it's masthead
Will be coming in"

— Nina Simone, Pirate Jenny

**Black Freighter Press** publishes revolutionary books.
committed to the exploration of liberation, using art
to transform consciousness. A platform for Black and
Brown writers to honor ancestry and propel radical
imagination.

CPSIA information can be obtained
at www.ICGtesting.com
Printed in the USA
JSHW061235120822
29194JS00002B/11